D0890675

Martin Zender's
Guide to
Intelligent Prayer

Also by Martin Zender

*How to Quit Church
Without Quitting God*

Martin Zender Goes To Hell

Flawed by Design

Martin Zender's Guide to
Intelligent
prayer

Do prayer circles work better
than prayer squares?

Martin Zender

STARKE & HARTMANN

Martin Zender's Guide to Intelligent Prayer

© 2004 by Martin Zender

Published by Starke & Hartmann
P.O. Box 6473
Canton, OH 44706
www.starkehartmann.com
1-866-866-BOOK

Printed in the United States of America

All rights reserved. No part of this publication may be reproduced, stored in a retrieval system, or transmitted in any form by any means, electronic, mechanical, photocopy, recording, or otherwise, without prior permission of the author, except as provided by USA copyright law.

ISBN 0-9709849-4-4

*To my wife,
who loves me
anyway*

ABOUT THE SCRIPTURE TRANSLATIONS
USED IN THIS BOOK

Whenever I quote scripture, accuracy is my first concern, but I also like paraphrased versions because of the relaxed language. I have struck a compromise. As long as the basic thought of the passage agrees with the more literal texts, I use J.B. Phillips' *The New Testament in Modern English.* But if Phillips blows it (and he often does) by sacrificing meaning for the sake of looser language, I quote from the *Concordant Literal New Testament* and the *Concordant Version of the Old Testament.* When it comes to accuracy, this is my version of choice. It's the translation I have found to be the most consistent in its uniform English renderings of Greek and Hebrew words. I quote from the *New American Standard Bible* occasionally; I like some of its Old Testament renderings. Whenever I need a more familiar frame of reference, I use the *King James Version* (KJV). But again, I do this only if the *KJV* happens to agree with the literal texts. I actually saw it happen once.

The New Testament in Modern English © J.B. Phillips

New American Standard Bible © The Lockman Foundation

Concordant Literal New Testament and *Concordant Version of the Old Testament* © Concordant Publishing Concern, 15570 Knochaven Rd., Santa Clarita, CA 91350

"And *this* is the boldness which we have toward Him, that if we should be requesting anything according to His will, He is hearing us."

—1 John 5:14,
*Concordant Literal
New Testament*

Once upon a time, a certain prayer warrior named Warren (it's a totally made-up name; I just invented it; his real name is Wally) wished for God to dampen a certain unholy occasion, namely, a local gay rights parade scheduled for the upcoming Saturday (Warren lived in Toronto). And so Warren sequestered himself in his bedroom, pulled the curtains, went to his knees, and implored the Deity in the following, whiney-like manner:

"God, please make it rain."

"No," said God from somewhere high above the CN Tower.

Warren was taken aback by God's directness. Forgetting he was imploring the Creator of the Universe, Warren followed up with, "Why not?" (Back in the old days, God might have opened a hole in Toronto and swallowed the audacious Warren into the subway system—or flushed him out into Lake Ontario—but this day God said):

"There aren't enough of you praying for it."

"How many do we need?"

"One-hundred forty-four thousand is a good number," replied God. "I like that number."

"Well, we've got twelve."

There was a moment of silence, repeated seven times. Warren began wondering if he'd lost his connection; he began wondering if he'd somehow insulted the Father of All. He was about to say, "God?…God?…" when there came the booming, celestial voice once again:

"Hm. Will everyone be closing their eyes?"

"Absolutely!" cried Warren, relieved.

"What about facial contortions?"

"Oh, that's easy enough." It was true. Many in Warren's prayer group, when they prayed, resembled people performing lateral deltoid raises with twenty-four pound dumbbells.

"I need at least one person to break a sweat and groan," said God in His angriest, most demanding tone.

Warren laughed out loud. "That would be Bill."

If God was taken aback by Warren's quick and easy response, He didn't let on. "Will you be holding hands?"

"What do *You* think?" said Warren, almost singing the words.

"I like hand-holding," said God wistfully.

"Oh, I know, I know."

"Boy-girl, boy-girl!" God boomed, recovering His frightening mien and snapping Warren back into fear mode. "And no funny stuff!"

"Yes, Lord!"

"When do you need it?"

"The rain, You mean?"

"No, the key to Atlantis. Of *course* the rain."

"Saturday, Lord."

"So—what? Is there a drought? A forest fire? What's happening down there?"

"There's a gay parade here on Saturday. Queers are taking over the earth."

"Hm. *That* figures. You're where again?"

"Toronto."

"Of course. Hm. Well, Saturday's going to be a problem."

"*What?*" Warren became whiney again, not that he'd ever really stopped. "Why?"

"Stop addressing Me in that tone!" demanded God. "There's a Methodist picnic up in Woodbridge. *Okay?*"

Warren's respect for the Deity waxed, then waned, then waxed, then waned again as he whined, "What the heck has that got to do with *anything!*"

God would have become angry and demolished that big dome thing where the Raptors played, but He considered the following information more devastating: "Oh, nothing. Just that the Methodists are petitioning Me fervently for it not to rain. *Fervently.* It's a formidable force up there in Woodbridge. They've bought a book on how to pray fervently. They got it at Barnes & Noble. It's called, *How To Pray Fervently.* I feel Myself caving in."

"But You're not caved in yet, are You?"

"No, not yet. They're still just looking at the pretty cover and reading the many endorsements on the back, written by respected theologians."

"Please, God. Can you tell me how many of the Methodists are praying for it not to rain?"

"Yes, I *can* tell you that. One hundred and seventeen souls, so far."

"We're doomed," lamented Warren.

God laughed out loud. "The hand-holding is going to help you, Mr. Whiney." God meant the nickname lovingly, but He knew the statement leading up to it would mystify Warren.

"You mean the Methodists aren't holding hands?"

God was taken aback. "I thought you'd be mystified by My words, but I see that you weren't—I mean, that you're not."

Warren tried to keep in mind how great God was. "How will this help us? Can You tell me?"

"You're nosey and audacious, but I like how you keep bugging Me. I'm going to let you in on a little secret. The only people I've ever told this to are Elijah and Oral Roberts. Four holding hands equals twenty not."

"Wow! I'm honored, God! What an advantage—to know this!"

"Don't tell anybody. I like things the way they are now."

"You can trust me. So twelve gives us…sixty. We're still short."

"And *still* you doubt the power of God; *still* you have not the faith of even a mustard seed. Did not I, Myself, bring the children of Israel through the Red Sea? Bill is going to groan and sweat. *Remember?*"

"Of course I remember."

"Well, he's worth fifty people."

"Wow! Am I only the third person to know this, too?"

"No, you're the fourth. I told Benny Hinn in 1983."

"Great! So that puts us at…one-ten. Still seven short."

"Eighteen short."

"*Huh?*"

"I just got eleven more 'no rains.'"

Warren slunk so dejectedly to the floor that his butt hit his heels, ruining his prayer pose. "We're sunk then," he whined from his slunk.

"Not necessarily. You could pull an all-nighter."

Warren shot back up into textbook form. "Are You talking about what I think You're talking about?"

God shrugged. "How should I know? What do you think I'm talking about?"

"I *think* You're talking about an all-night prayer vigil," answered Warren.

"Well," said God, "then I guess you *were* thinking about what I was talking about."

"I hear those work mystically good."

"Mystically *well*," corrected God. "Mystically *well*."

"Do we all have to do it?"

"One equals six after ten p.m. And one equals twelve after midnight."

"So two after midnight will put us over."

"Or My name isn't unpronounceable by Jewish people."

"I guess I could do it with Rob."

"I don't think so, Smugnuts." God addressed Warren with an endearing yet humiliating nickname of His own creation.

"Why not?" asked Warren, hardly believing that the Deity had just called him "Smugnuts."

"Rob works midnights; he's too used to it."

Warren groaned. "We have to suffer?"

"I'm partial to suffering. Hello? Read Leviticus."

"What if Rob stays up and prays all day?"

"Hello? No!"

"Look, I'll just try to come up with someone else."

"I'll give you Rob during the day if he kneels."

"We were going to kneel anyway."

"Now you tell Me."

"I thought You knew."

"One kneeling equals five standing. And you're the first one I've *ever* told this."

"Awesome!"

"Will you be using padded kneelers?" asked God.

"Our church doesn't have them," answered Warren.

"Then one equals eight."

"Ah! The suffering factor."

"Not so fast. You've got trouble. Pastor Pete's heading for his prayer closet."

"Who's Pastor Pete?"

"Hello? Grand Poo-Bah, Ninth Street Methodist Church of God; Ninth Street Methodist Church of *Me*."

"But he's only one guy."

"But he's got more degrees than Nebuchadnezzar's oven."

"So?"

"We're talking A.B., M.Div., M.Th., D.D., D.Sac.Lit., PhD., Litt.D, D.Sac. Theol. That's what we're talking here. Have you ever seen more capital and small letters mixed together?"

"We're sunk—is that what You're saying, Lord?"

"I'm not saying that."

"Then…"

"He's fat. Pete is fat. He's eating a Ding Dong as we speak."

Warren felt a flicker of hope. "In his prayer closet?"

"This is what I'm telling you."

"What can we do?"

"You can fast."

"Why did I know You were going to say that?"

"I love it when people don't eat. It twists My arm that much harder."

"So how long do we have to starve ourselves?"

"Twenty-four hours, minimum."

"We'll have to think about it."

"Time's up. Do you want to soak the homos, or don't you?"

"Sure, but..."

"Then I need a commitment."

"I don't know. Look—what do *You* want to do?"

God fell down, got back up, fell down again, then recovered before any of His attending angels could bat a wing and ask what had happened. "I'm sorry," God said, "but what did you just ask Me, Warren? It sounded like you wanted to know what *I* wanted to do."

"I did."

God stroked His beard so fast and so thoroughly that many of the attending angels thought it might catch fire. "Amazing," said God. "I haven't been asked that question in two thousand and fifteen years."

"Seriously."

"I kid you not."

"Well, I'm asking it now. What do You want?"

"Honestly? I was planning rain."

"Oh."

"In fact, I've had rain planned for Saturday for ten thousand years."

"Well. Okay. Then I guess the twelve of us really don't need to—"

"Don't get lazy on Me!"

"Okay!"

"Uh-oh."

"What's wrong, Lord?"

"The Methodists are forming a circle."

"I hope it's not a—"

"Yes! It's a prayer circle."

"They're reading the book?"

"Chapter twelve. Ho! It's shaping up to be a beauty."

"We're finished then."

"I'm sorry, Warren, but this one is very, *very* round."

"Lord! Is there anything we can do?"

"Nothing. I'm generally helpless against these...I...*I'm being pulled toward the circle!*"

"God! Wait!"

"Such roundness! Help!"

"God! Come back!"

"NOOOOOOooooooooooooooooo!"

He is unique and who can turn Him?
                —Job 23:13
"My purpose will be established."
                —Isaiah 46:10

The Glory of Israel will not lie or change His mind.
                —1 Samuel 15:29
"I have planned it, surely I will do it."
                —Isaiah 46:11

He is not a man that He should change His mind.
                —1 Samuel 15:29
"For I, the Lord, do not change."
                —Malachi 3:6

For the Lord of Hosts has planned, and who can frustrate it?
                —Isaiah 14:27
"I will accomplish all My good pleasure."
                —Isaiah 46:10

And what His soul desires, that He does.
                —Job 23:13
"There is no one like me, declaring the end from the beginning."
                —Isaiah 46:9-10

As for His stretched-out hand, who can turn it back?
 —Isaiah 14:27
"Is My hand so short that it cannot ransom?"
 —Isaiah 50:2

These are just a few of the verses showing God running the universe apart from human wheedling. Pull up a stool and read these verses again. If you're already sitting down, lie down; everything is going to be all right. God listens to everyone, but He acts in accord with His own predetermined course, a course that makes our courses look puny and primitive. Then what is prayer? First let us say in twelve words or less what prayer is not.

Prayer is not the hand that moves the hand of God.

What is it? Prayer is the desire for God's will to be done.

The New Testament writers wrote and spoke in Greek. The word they used to describe communication with the Deity (the Greek word that has been translated "prayer") was *proseuche*. The New Testament folks never prayed, ever. They *proseuche-ed*. What did this word mean to them? That's a good question. No one has asked it in two thousand and fifteen years.

Proseuche is a three-part word. The prefix *pros* is TOWARD, *eu* means WELL, and the rest of the word is, HAVING.

Prayer, then, is literally TOWARD-WELL-HAVING. Toward whose well-having? Think of who you pray to. You pray to God. So according to the building blocks of this word, prayer is whatever would promote the well-having of God, i.e., "Thy will be done."

But how many pray this way? Most people want their will to be done, not God's. (Some people even think—listen to this—that their will *is* God's will.) That is, they want their own well-having. What happens when human well-having clashes with the divine variety? If you have caught even a whiff of the greatness of God, you already know the answer.

God wins.

Would you really want it any other way? Could you bear the pressure or the consequence of God enacting your whims? Here is comforting news: Whenever a human will goes up against the divine will and clashes with it, the human will mercifully loses. Or should I say it wins. God knows best what all of us need. This is because He is a tad smarter than we are. Is this a revelation? It is to some people.

Does God always do what's best for humanity? The answer is, Yes. Since He is a benevolent God, His well-have is the best for everyone. It doesn't always seem this way, I realize that. How can God be doing what is best for you if you're dying of cancer? If your child is sick? If your spouse has just left you? I don't know, but He is.

It's a trust thing. Since God is God, and since God is love, He has to know what He's doing, and it has to work toward everyone's ultimate good; "ultimate" is the key word here. It will be the best thing in the long run.

In the short run, God does hard things, well do I know this. I hate this life sometimes, so don't think you own the franchise on sin and/or discouragement. In my agony, I cry out to God when the pain becomes too much. I have even damned out loud His intermediate plans for my life. So if I have not been struck by lightning yet—and I haven't—then you should be living a life relatively free of worry. I love God, I just buck His system sometimes. Can I admit to you that I have even thrown things at the Almighty? Okay, then I won't. But it's hard to take the universe upon one's shoulders, even harder to hit the Deity with a pine cone. If I had the choice, I would choose the easiest course for myself. So thank God I don't have the choice. I don't know what's good for me. I'm like the child who would pray for chocolate chip cookies and a Mountain Dew for supper. But God makes me eat my broccoli. When I've got the griping out of my system, I eventually shut up, sit down, and resume the mantel of creaturehood.

It's much more relaxing this way.

In spite of how everything looks now, I have learned to trust God. Something great is going to happen that will justify every bad thing. I know this to be true. Knowing that God will eventually exceed my expectations, I can sort-of bear what often looks like hopeless chaos to me. But none of it is hopeless chaos; it only looks that way. God is not the author of chaos.

I've learned about prayer the hard way. After 1) babbling like a baby, 2) failing to convince God to enact my whims, and 3) wondering what went wrong (Am I not spiritual enough? Should I have prayed longer?

Here's a photo of the actual pine cone I threw at God. I missed.

Should I maybe not have thrown that pine cone at Him?), I've finally figured out that there's only one God and I'm not Him. On the heels of this revelation came the thought that God has a huge plan that will turn out perfectly in the end, even though some of the interim heartache will make me cry. But when His plan is finished I will say, "You are a genius, God, and a righteous Father. I see now why You did what You did. It didn't make sense then, but it makes a lot of sense now, since this is what You were working toward. I'm sorry I said so many bad words, but I was a weak human being then and You have to admit You kept a lot of glory from the range of my perception."

And God will say, "I admit it. Relax. You couldn't have handled the glory anyway. I made you how you were and it kept you humble, didn't it? Kept you weak? Okay. So how much time did you waste worrying? What made you think I'd be mad at you after sending My Son to represent you before Me?"

If prayer changed things, we'd all be in trouble. Imagine eight-billion people storming heaven simultaneously. Imagine God throwing His papers all around and wondering what to do, who to answer. Imagine God finally plugging His ears and grinding His pearly white teeth in holy exasperation. This is a worse scenario than if God just ignored us all and continued with His plan, which He came up with quite a long time ago when everything was calm and peaceful and humanity had not been invented. I suppose God could concentrate better back then, without everyone "storming heaven" with their prayers and "breaking through" to the blessed life. His plan is for our benefit, anyway. You must believe this, in spite of what the clergy say.

Here is God's plan:

God has allowed us to know the secret of his plan and it is this: he purposed long ago in his sovereign will that all human history should be consummated in Christ, that everything that exists in Heaven or earth should find its perfection and fulfillment in him.

—*the Apostle Paul,* Ephesians 1:9-10

Here it is again, in another place:

Christ is the visible expression of the invisible God...It was in him that the full nature of God chose to live, and through him God planned to reconcile to his own person everything on earth and everything in Heaven, making peace by virtue of Christ's death on the cross.

—*the Apostle Paul,* Colossians 1:15, 19-20

I know that these two verses have just destroyed about a dozen Christian creeds, and I do admit that I love it when that happens. If creeds clash with scriptural truth, I say get rid of the creeds. Two of the creeds just destroyed are eternal torment and eternal death for all unchurched sinners. If you believe in either eternal torment or eternal death, then you cannot believe God will realize the grand plan just detailed. Because how is someone you love getting tortured for eternity in any way the working out of an almighty, glorious plan? How would it align with these two passages of scripture?

I think that many of my readers have perhaps gone into this prayer thing assuming certain awful things about God that just aren't true. For one thing, you haven't trusted God. How can you trust Him if you believe He is so crazy that He would burn someone in the orthodox version of hell for eternity? How *can* you pray for God's well-have, when His well-have might include sending your son, your husband, your daughter, or your mother to an eternity of torment? God obviously has a temper problem that causes Him to punish people way out of proportion to their sin. And this, after He supposedly sent a perfect sacrifice for that sin.

No wonder you haven't trusted God enough to pray for His well-have. In the back of your mind, God is untrustable and unstable. Can you admit this? Deep down, you have considered Him a short-tempered, frightening Deity. You haven't had the courage to question Him honestly, or say contrary things to Him out loud. Maybe you are not yet as unreligious as I am. Or perhaps you're a choir director. But this questioning of God's character sticks deep down in your soul. And so you have prayed, prayed, and prayed toward *your* well-have, because not even you would torment anyone for eternity, not even a McDonalds cashier. So you must be more levelheaded and loving than God. Because of this, you have trusted yourself with prayer, and not God.

But once you get true things in your mind about God, you'll be able to better understand what He's doing, and you will stop trusting yourself. Not that you'll be ecstatic with everything God does, but you won't lose your mind and your peace so readily. You'll still cry, but you'll cry intelligently and not with so much desperation and fear.

Some people don't know what's good for them.

Hi.

About 23 years ago, I thought I wanted to marry a girl named Erica. Not only did Erica have a great personality, she had Bette Davis eyes and several Jean Harlow characteristics. I figured Erica and I would have at least five children, and would I ever enjoy the process. I prayed and prayed to God to let me marry Erica. But God broke my heart by having Erica marry Edward. (*Edward*, of all people.)

Then I met Melody. And when I met Melody I said to God, "God, You're a genius. You had someone better for me all along. Thank You for not answering my selfish prayer." And God just smiled and said, "You're just now figuring that out?" And I said, "Well, I am pretty slow." And God said, "I know better than you what you need. My view is so much better than yours." And I said, "Thanks for overriding me and taking the long view." And God said, "I invented the long view. Would you want it any other way?" And I said, very quickly, "No!"

Jesus Christ is a better example of this. The closer He got to the cross, the more He panicked. He had human emotions and glands, so as He got closer to the agony of the cross—as close as the night before it—He cried out and prayed to God that, if there were some other way, He would deliver Him from the terrible cross:

Then Jesus came with the disciples to a place called Gethsemane and said to them, "Sit down here while I go over there and pray."

Then he took with him Peter and the two sons of Zebedee and began to be in terrible pain and agony of mind.

"My heart is breaking with a deathlike grief," he told them, "stay here and keep watch with me."

Then he walked on a little way and fell on his face and prayed, "My Father, if it is possible let this cup pass from me."

I cry at this myself. It hurts so badly to think of Jesus suffering this way. But here was a prayer. *Here was a prayer!* And yet the greatest prayer followed:

"Yet it must not be what I want, but what you want."
—Matthew 26:36-39

That was the greatest prayer ever uttered. Why pray the prayer of Jabez when you can pray the prayer of Jesus? The prayer of Jabez was an immature plea uttered by a man who wanted more personal territory and a relatively evil-free life. God inspired Jabez to pray this prayer—it's true—and God answered it. It was the right prayer for the time, even if it was immature. There is a time for immaturity. We were all babies once, and that's fine. It's fine to eat beet mush as long as you're not committed to it forever.

The reason *The Prayer of Jabez*, by Bruce Wilkinson, has sold so many copies is that it caters to modern Americans with the "I-want-an-awesome-life" mindset who crave 1) more personal territory, 2) a relatively evil-free existence, and 3) the satisfaction of having earned it by concentrated, daily effort. COMFORT AND PERSONAL ACCOMPLISHMENT FIRST, SPIRITUAL MATURITY SECOND is the battle cry of this generation, especially should maturity involve less personal territory and, say, a toothache.

Do you want to become mature in your prayer life? Then pray the prayer of Jesus: "Yet it must not be what I want, but what You want."

This is probably the hardest prayer to pray. But in terms of maturity, it's way ahead of Jabez. It's all about letting go and trusting God.

It was God's will that Jesus should die. I think Jesus knew that; He just didn't like it. I didn't like it when God snatched my girlfriend away and gave her to Edward. God did not expand my borders, and neither did He keep me from evil. But God's wisdom was justified when I met Melody. And look how God's wisdom was justified with His Son, when God:

> ...raised him from the dead and gave him the place of highest honour in Heaven—a place that is infinitely superior to any command, authority, power or control, and which carries with it a name far beyond any name that could ever be used in this world or the world to come.
>
> God has placed everything under the power of Christ
> —Ephesians 1:20-22.

Thank God that Jesus did not pray the prayer of Jabez.

I had this friend one time with political bumper stickers all over his car. The amazing thing was that every candidate this guy ever slapped on his car bumper, won. His track record was so amazing that I thought he was either into tarot cards or had just waxed his Ouija board. I finally asked him how he did it and he said: "I put the bumper stickers on *after* the elections."

Mark Twain once said, "When I was a boy of fourteen, my father was so ignorant I could hardly stand to have the old man around. But when I got to be twenty-one, I was astonished at how much he had learned in seven years."

The longer people walk with God, the more they shut up and listen to those who are smarter than they are. Shutting up, they hear better. Hearing better, they learn. Learning, they buy the right bumper stickers. Buying the right bumper stickers, they pray and appear as geniuses. Or at least very spiritual. Because when one prays for what God wants, it always happens.

Always.

Consider Elijah:

Tremendous power is made available through a good man's earnest prayer. Do you remember Elijah? He was a man as human as we are but he prayed earnestly that it should not rain. In fact, not a drop fell on the land for three and a half years. Then he prayed again, the heavens gave the rain and the earth sprouted with vegetation again.

—James 5:17-18

Elijah was the poster boy for prayer long before Jabez became a Christian pop star. But the prophet would deny all credit. "Why are you putting me on a pedestal?" Elijah would say. "I had no great 'prayer power.' All I did was listen to God." And he refers us to the following:

> Now Elijah the Tishbite, who was of the settlers of Gilead, said to Ahab, "As the Lord, the God of Israel lives, before whom I stand, surely there shall be neither dew nor rain these years, except by my word."
> —1 Kings 17:1

"That's the secret," Elijah says. "I said the prayer, yes, but the information came from God. I stood before the living God, and here is where I learned when the rain would stop."

"But what about when it returned?" we would want to know. "James says you prayed again and the heavens gave rain."

"James is talking about effects, not causes. He's correct. That's what happened. But there was a cause before the effect that James doesn't mention. The book of First Kings lays it out." And he shares with us this:

> Now it came about after many days, that the word of the Lord came to Elijah in the third year, saying, "Go, show

yourself to Ahab, and I will send rain on the face of the earth."

—1 Kings 18:1

"Where has *that* verse been?" we would ask.

"Oh, it's been there."

"So the word of the Lord came to you first, *then* you prayed?"

"Yes. James does make me look good. He says, 'Elijah prayed, and the rain came.' True enough. I prayed and it rained. James just didn't mention what went before. He didn't reference 1 Kings 18:1. God whispered His counsel, *then* I prayed. I'm no genius, just a good listener."

Ever hear the story of the foreign explorers who got captured by natives? These particular natives were frighteningly 1) naked, 2) boned through their noses, and 3) engaged in boiling seven National Geographic photographers on the back burner.

The explorers were terrified, but they were also smart. They knew that a solar eclipse was to occur the following day, so they devised a plan. They told the natives (in international sign language): "If you no let us go, we take sun away tomorrow, when little hand on three and big hand on twelve. Then you know our mighty power. Then you let us go."

The natives said: "It is the dung of cheetahs, what you say about sun. Nobody do that. We *eat* you tomorrow."

So the explorers said: "Wait and see, Bone-noses. We prove our great power tomorrow, when little hand on three and big hand on twelve."

So the next day, at 2:59 p.m., the explorers made a tremendous hoopla at the sun. They yelled at the sun in mystical languages. This hoopla included New York-style tap dancing and not a few somersaults. Their timing in all this was impeccable because they had their wristwatches on and had read Carl Sagan's article in the previous day's *Times*.

And guess what? As soon as the explorers finished their hoopla, the sun went away. This made the natives pee briskly into their banana peels. Soon after (one might say "immediately"), the natives let everybody go.

Advice of the day: Find out what's going to happen, *then* pray.

The hoopla included New York-style tap dancing.

When he did ask people to pray, the apostle Paul never asked them to pray for it not to rain during church picnics or evangelistic crusades. He asked people to pray intelligently for things he already knew would happen. For example, in a letter from Rome to his friends in Ephesus, Paul wrote, "Pray for me, too, that I may be able to speak the message here boldly" (Ephesians 6:19). It was no trick when this prayer came to pass, because God told Paul before he even got to Rome, "Take heart!—for as you have witnessed boldly for me in Jerusalem, so you must give your witness for me in Rome" (Acts 23:11).

The Ephesians might have said, "But Paul. You already said it was God's plan for you to speak boldly in Rome. Why are you now asking us to pray that you speak boldly in Rome?" And Paul might have answered, "It will just make me feel good to know you're praying for me. And as long as you're praying, you may as well pray intelligently."

You will find many places in scripture where prayer seems suspenseful. In some places, there are formulas God gives that, if people pray a certain way, God will do a certain thing. It appears in some places that God is waiting for people to ask Him, to inform Him, to beg

Him, to command Him. I know about these passages and I believe every one of them. But—

We are seeing effects, not causes. We are looking through knotholes, not over the fence. God says, "You pray for *this* and I'll do *that*." Yes. I believe it. But look above the stage and you'll see *wh*y the people are praying: God is moving them to pray. He is causing them to participate in His plans. He whispers His plans to their subconscious minds, and the prayers follow. (This is why one person in tune with God prays better than ten thousand perspiring "prayer warriors" who are out of sync with Him.) Scripture doesn't always let us in on this "God-puts-it-on-the-heart" aspect, but it's always there. Do you really think God's plans hinge on human cooperation? On the number of people praying? On the length of their petitions? Do you really think God needs human beings telling Him what's going on? Waking Him up?

I'm not inventing this "God-moves-people" thing. Here is one place where scripture does reveal God's hand. God to Israel:

"In the day I cleanse you from all your depravities, then I cause the cities to be indwelt, and built shall be the deserted places. And the desolated land shall be served, whereas it had become a desolation to the eyes of everyone passing by.

"Then know shall the nations, which are remaining

round about you, that I, Yahweh, I build the demolished, I plant the desolated, I, Yahweh, I speak and I do it."

Thus says my Lord Yahweh: *"Further, for this shall I be inquired of by the house of Israel, to do it for them."*
—Ezekiel 36:33-34, 37

When my kids were little, I used to tell them, "You guys are going to bed at nine o'clock tonight." It was my son Aaron who always asked, "How can *you* tell?"

God says, "For this *shall* I be inquired of by the house of Israel." And the Christians who think prayer is the hand that moves the hand of God say, "But God, how can *You* tell?"

Gee, I don't know. Maybe He can tell because He's God. Maybe He can tell because He's ordering the universe and all its inhabitants. Maybe He can tell because He devised a great plan before any of us were born and nothing can deflect it. Maybe He can tell because He is the cause behind all inquiring, and He plants all the little bugs in our ears that cause us to pray for what He has already decided should occur.

But maybe, just maybe, God is gracious enough to let us participate in His plan. Maybe He gives us prayers to make us involved with what He's already purposed to do. Maybe He's like the father who lets the child touch the steering wheel of the car occasionally. The kid's driving! Well, no. But he is participating.

The ignorance! The ignorance of people who think: *We moved God*, or: *We broke through to the blessed life*; proud, small people who embrace the relative and ignore the absolute; who drool at the knothole and never become mature enough to look over the fence. I challenge these people: Wake up to your creaturehood and expand your view. You do not move God, He moves you. Prayer doesn't move God, God moves prayer. See the big picture. You are not driving the car, you are participating in the journey. Snap out of it; you're merely touching the steering wheel of God's car.

Be thankful that God even lets you touch the wheel. But don't be dumb. If God is going to Boston, no amount of wheel-yanking will get you to New York. So rest and ask God: "Where are You going?" You will be amazed at how slick your prayers will become after this. The apostle John puts it very simply, and this verse sums up everything I've been saying:

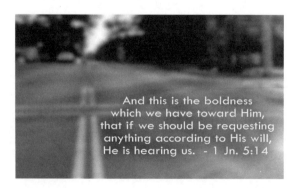

And this is the boldness which we have toward Him, that if we should be requesting anything according to His will, He is hearing us. - 1 Jn. 5:14

A parable

God's will is a 45 mile stretch of Amtrak railway linking Washington D.C. and Baltimore. I board the Silver Bullet in Baltimore at 8:15 a.m.

The Engineer is distributing pamphlets to each passenger, and mine accompanies me to a window seat three rows behind the control room. Reading light is poor in town, but as we snake out of Baltimore, rural Maryland returns the sun. I unfold my pamphlet and read. The pamphlet says:

IF YOU REQUEST ANY VIEW ACCORDING TO THIS ROUTE, YOU WILL SEE IT - *The Engineer.*

I smile. This is typical of an Engineer Who practically invented this route. He likes inviting view-requests because He wants His out-of-state guests to have the same appreciation that He, Himself, holds for this scenic passage.

I've lived in Baltimore and worked in Washington long enough to have memorized the highlights along this familiar stretch of rail. I know, for instance, that the FCC monitoring station, with its high towers and radio dishes (a possible point of interest to visitors) will appear out the right window three minutes south of

Harwood Park terminal. We're just about there.

"Engineer? May we see the FCC monitoring station?"

I make His day. "Sure can," He says. "Just ahead and to the right."

Thirty noses still steam the glass long after the monitoring station has passed from view. Which passenger will speak next?

We're passing through Annapolis Junction, and the Patuxent National Wildlife Refuge will appear on the left. It's a pretty good tourist draw. No one else is requesting a view, so I speak up again.

"Engineer? May we see the Patuxent National Wildlife Refuge?"

I can almost hear Him smiling. "Here it comes now," He says, gesturing toward the East. "And if you'll look closely over near that brown fence, you may see deer. We saw about fifteen of them there yesterday." Everybody is looking for deer. "Oh, I see one!" says an elderly woman in a pink hat. "Where?" asks a gentleman beside her. The passengers are loosening up.

I learn that Pink Hat is president of the Ladies Historical Society of Braintree, a suburb of Boston, and is on her way to Washington to visit her sister. Pink Hat has a request.

"Yoo-hoo! Engineer! Isn't Frances Scott Key's birthplace is Maryland? Could we see it?"

I'm shaking my head. No, lady. Frances Scott Key's birthplace isn't on this route. It's near Taneytown, eight miles from the Pennsylvania line.

Engineer knows that, of course, and maintains silent vigil on the track. Pink Hat is obviously disappointed; I can hear her grating her dentures.

There's a guy from Pottstown, Pennsylvania, wearing bib overalls, sitting in the aisle seat across from me. He's heading to Washington for a farmer's rally at the Capitol. Now he, too, has a request.

"Hey! Engineer! Ain't the Carroll County Farm Museum somewhere near here? God, I'd love to lay my eyes on that."

Forget it, I think. The Carroll County Farm Museum is in Carroll county, some thirty-five miles to the northwest. I don't like Overalls' tone, and I hope the Engineer says something to appease him. He doesn't. I try to sink a couple inches into my shirt collar.

Overalls misinterprets the silence from headquarters as haughty indifference. Since he has no dentures to grate, Overalls settles for the nerves of the passengers and exercises his right to speak without thinking.

"Engineer!" He is practically bellowing. "Didn't you hear me? I said I wanted to see the Carroll County Farm Museum!"

The farmer's belligerence warrants no response from headquarters, and that's exactly what he gets. Hopefully, he will forget about the farm museum. He does not.

Overalls is now pivoting his bulk in the narrow aisle, standing as tall as he is wide, straining to draw a breath big enough to address his trainmates. As for me, I'm half-way down the seat.

"Now, lookie *here!*" Overalls huffs, addressing the astonished passengers. "How many of y'uns want to see the Carroll County Farm Museum?"

Pink Hat raises her hand. The guy sitting next to Overalls raises his. Soon, hands spring up everywhere. This dull but imposing Pottstownian has somehow managed to muster a troop around his pet cause. Encouraged, he tosses a thumb toward the control room. "Obviously, folks, Engineer ain't heard us. But I'll bet that if we get together on this and shout loud enough and long enough, Engineer'll *hafta* show us the Carroll County Farm Museum."

Now I've got my knees drawn up to my ears. Hadn't these people read their pamphlets? *According to this route*, the pamphlet said. Let your requests be made *according to this route*. If that wasn't enough, there was a section of the pamphlet that listed notable sights *on* the route. Why hadn't the passengers acquainted themselves with it? Had they done so, they would have been able to request their views intelligently, and the Engineer would surely have granted them. But now, this.

The passengers seemed to be losing their heads. If

"Hey! Let's see Mount Rushmore!"

the Carroll County Farm Museum had been on the route, didn't they think the Engineer would have delivered as promised? But now, the awful chant begins. Overalls starts it, several of the men give it strength, and Pink Hat contributes a sickly soprano overtone:

CARROLL COUNTY *FARM* MUSEUM!
CARROLL COUNTY *FARM* MUSEUM!
CARROLL COUNTY *FARM* MUSEUM!

It would serve them all right if Engineer threw the brakes and made them all walk to Washington. But Engineer's patience is legendary. I am wondering what He will do. Will He switch tracks at College Park and run the northwest line into Carroll county? I doubted it. He enjoyed granting view requests, but I had never known Him to switch tracks to do it. Will He flash His Engineer's badge and pull rank? He could. *I* would.

Engineer does nothing—and it works. The manmade mantra is self-destructing. The mantra's disciples are falling through the holes in their own script. Obviously, a visit to the Carroll County Farm Museum is not on this train's itinerary, and no amount of intercessory gymnastics, however sweaty, will put it there. Soon, only Overalls and Pink Hat can be heard above the rhythmic clack of the wheels. But Overalls is losing his wind, Pink Hat her dentures. Finally, even they surrender to the will of the rails.

CEASE STRIVING, AND KNOW THAT I AM GOD—Ps. 46:10

Suddenly, Engineer does a 180 degree turn in His swivel chair. He's gonna kill Overalls! No. Instead, He addresses the fat farmer as a friend. "Overalls! Did you know that the USDA has an agricultural research service in Beltsville?"

Overalls is stunned. "No kiddin'? Whoa! Are we goin' through there?"

"*Right* through there."

"Hot dang! In that case, can we see the USDA Agricultural Research Service?"

"We may, and thanks for a fine request."

Next, Engineer addresses Pink Hat, who is fussing with a tube of Fixodent. "Pink Hat!"

The startled grandmother leaps to attention.

"Did you know that Frances Scott Key had a law office in the District of Columbia?"

"Oh, well, actually, I...reeeeally?"

"Really. Would you like to see it? We'll be going right by it on our way to Union Station."

"Why, yes. I *would* like to see that."

"Request granted."

* * *

AND THIS IS THE BOLDNESS WHICH WE
HAVE TOWARD HIM, THAT IF WE SHOULD BE
REQUESTING ANYTHING ACCORDING TO
HIS WILL, HE IS HEARING US. 1 Jn. 5:14

My flaws had become too much for me, and I writhed on the living room floor before God. I prayed that He would kill me. Better death, I thought, than another minute of imperfection. So I cried and prayed, begging Him for a change of life. All I wanted was to be a better person.

Then it happened. Rarely has a prayer been answered so quickly, and so completely. As I lay with my face to Earth, the words came distinctly from the throne of heaven:

"Get up. My grace is sufficient for you."

That was the revolution. So simple, and yet, in that moment, my life changed forever. I did not rise from the floor with any fewer sins; I arose with the knowledge that sin could never condemn me. I arose knowing that He had heard me, that He cared for me, and that in all my imperfections He was there with more than enough grace.

The lesson? Pray. Pray wildly if you have to. If your heart is breaking, don't try to fashion your words or pray intelligently. Just pour out your heart to God. This is my recommendation even if you do have specific and selfish requests. In Philippians 4:6, the apostle Paul says: "In everything, by prayer and petition, with thanksgiving, let your requests be made known to God." How can you be thankful for trouble? You can't, at least not while you're going through it. In this context, however, I believe the thing you're supposed to be thankful for is the opportunity to lay your worry on God. Because look at the very next thing Paul says: "Do not worry about anything."

There's a revolution for you. As if that's not enough, the next verse slams home the point on this type of "request" praying: "And then the peace of God, that is superior to every frame of mind, shall be garrisoning your hearts and your apprehensions in Christ Jesus." In other words, making your requests known is designed to give you peace, not the thing you request. Otherwise, Paul would have said, "Make your requests known, and God will grant them." The requests serve to unburden you, and this is what brings the peace and the worry-free mindset. You can then think to yourself, *Okay. I gave it to God. What more can I do? The ball is in His court now. I'm going to get up off this floor and go out for a hamburger.* We request things to unburden ourselves, not to get what we want. If your request is in accord with God's will, you will get what you want. If it's not, you won't. Maybe by the next day you will be able to say, "Not my will, but Thine be done."

That will be soon enough.

Yet another parable

There is in Jerusalem near the sheep-pens a pool surrounded by five arches, which has the Hebrew name of Bethzatha. Under these arches a great many sick people were in the habit of lying; some of them were blind, some lame, and some had withered limbs. (They used to wait there for the "moving of the water," for at certain times an angel used to come down into the pool and disturb the water, and then the first person who stepped into the water after the disturbance would be healed of whatever he was suffering from.)

—This paragraph compliments of John 5:2-4 from The *New Testament in Modern English*

There is also at this time, in Jerusalem, a man from Tulsa, Oklahoma—a "healer"—who can hardly believe there can be this many stupid people crammed beneath five arches. He approaches a human-shaped lump with a withered limb and demands the reason for it (the withered limb, that is.)

"I was born this way," the woman says.

"No," says the healer. "I mean, why is it still this way?"

"I can't get to the water."

"What's with the water?"

"An angel comes down at certain times and stirs up the water. First one in gets healed."

"What certain times? What do you mean, 'certain times?'"

"Nothing regular. Sometimes once a month, sometimes once a year. Five years ago we had three in one day. I think we're due for something like that again. Naomi says that the Gorazin brothers say that—"

"Wait a minute. You mean the angel comes down whenever he feels like it?"

"You said that, not me. I would never say anything like that."

"Why not?"

"I don't push angels. You're messing with angels, Mister. Angels do what they want, when they want. I actually saw the angel that came here in '14. Now, I wouldn't be the one to tell him to get a move on."

"Well maybe the angel needs to take a closer look at what's going on down here. What does this mass of withered humanity do to the glory of God? Do you ever think in those terms, or have you been lulled into a spiritual stupor? Some people mistake spiritual stupors for patience, you know."

"Oh, I see. You think I'm one of those people. For your information, I'm not one and I never could be. I'm very patient. In fact—see that lady over there with the sideways head? That's Hilda. She says I have the patience of Job."

"Oh. Right. At least Job complained. Do you ever complain?"

"Sure I complain. But it doesn't put me out of my hope. I don't know about what you say. I think you're wrong. Job was a 'wretched mass,' and God was glorified in him."

"How?"

"Job learned patience through the things he suffered. He saw that God was everything and he was nothing. God blessed Job in the end."

"In the *end*. Meanwhile, you have unlimited spiritual power at your disposal and you're not using it."

With that, the healer left the woman to accost a blind man.

"Who is this accosting me?" asked the blind man.

"Call me the Answer to Your Immediate Vision Difficulties. How long have you been hanging around this morgue?"

"Twenty-nine years."

"How old are you?"

"Twenty-nine."

"Blind all this time?"

"Yep."

"Never seen anything."

"Nope."

"And you're waiting for—"

"The angel. The angel comes to stir the water, and..."

"I've heard. First one in gets healed, that is, *if* the angel shows up."

"It happens. Besides, the Gorazin brothers say we're due."

"I'm sure that just makes you feel peachy, you, sitting here ninety feet from the edge of the pool with four million people in front of you."

"Ninety feet? Don't kid me, Mister. Missy 'Lizabeth told me I was up near the front."

"Ten years ago maybe. You're at least ninety feet out now."

"Well...hmm...*shoo!* I don't care. Something's going to work out."

"Work out? For who? For the one person out of six million who's well enough to get to the water first? What about the five million, nine-hundred ninety nine thousand who wait until God-knows-when for the angel to come back? How does it work out for them? How has it worked out for you in the last twenty-nine years?"

"Stop talking like that."

"Patience is one thing, stupidity is another."

"You're a lot of help."

"Do you even want to see?"

"I haven't been hanging out here for the tan."

"Then just believe. Have faith."

"Okay...now what?"

"What do you mean, 'Now what?'"

"I just believed and had faith. But hot damn, I still can't see. Got a Plan B?"

"Oh, for God's sake. You call that having faith?"

"How do you know how much faith I just had?"

"You didn't wince, or scream, or break into a sweat. You didn't roll down the aisle."

"Oh, no. I kicked the booze five years ago."

"Oh. Okay. So this is one big joke to you. Well then, you deserve to sit here for another twenty-nine years. And if you do, you'll have no one to blame for it but yourself and your lack of faith."

"Listen, Preach. Faith is a gift of God. I have what I have. If I don't have any more, what can I do about it? I can't manufacture it. Cripe, I can't even see. All I know is, if I can get into the water when the angel stirs it, I'll see again. If I don't, I won't."

"And you're satisfied with that?"

"I've learned to rest in it and be at peace. I want to be healed, but I don't worry about it."

"You're a fatalist."

"No, Preach. Just a realist. You'd be surprised what I *do* see. I have many spiritual blessings—many. And spiritual blessings—you don't need eyes for those. Besides, my blindness will last only as long as my life in this body. There ain't no blind people in the resurrection.

This life is not all there is, and you should know that. This life is short. I look forward so much to the resurrection. I bet I look forward to it more than you. You're on some big roll with your big plans. Me? I'm waiting for Messiah—this afternoon would be good. *My* plans? To hell with them. All I want is Messiah. In the meantime, I have all this fellowship here, with all these people who have faith like me. Faith sustains us. Faith is a conviction about things that aren't seen. Think about that, Preach. If I could see, I wouldn't need faith, now would I? If I were healed today, my faith would disappear. Faith can only thrive in lack. Don't you get that? Faith is *not* receiving. There's a special kind of joy in that."

With these words, the healer strode off with a curse, at the same time shielding his eyes from the warm Jerusalem sun.

Faith is not receiving.

Who made Shirley Dobson my prayer captain? I didn't. I didn't even get to vote. Had I been asked, I would have voted for Jesus Christ. But there was Shirley Dobson on the cover of *Focus on the Family* magazine. The words on the cover, next to Shirley's picture said:

Shirley Dobson: Captain of America's Prayer Force.

But then it hit me how nice Shirley was. I rejoiced. If I did not live in America, Shirley Dobson would not be my Prayer Captain. If I lived in Cuba, Fidel Castro might be my Prayer Captain and I would be afraid. Shirley is gentle and kind and very pretty, whereas Fidel Castro has many serious personality flaws and a bushy beard that inspires fear.

I suddenly felt blessed.

The *Focus on the Family* magazine I speak of appeared in February of 1994. But as I write, Shirley Dobson is still forcing American prayers to heaven. I can't imagine what kind of pressure Shirley has been struggling under these past years. I wonder what it is doing to her. I haven't seen any recent pictures of Shirley, but she must look like Phyllis Diller by now.

But this is not all. Not only is Shirley Dobson the Captain of America's Prayer Force, she also chairs the National Day of Prayer. This is an incredible responsi-

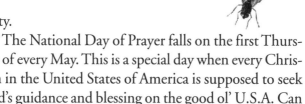

bility.

The National Day of Prayer falls on the first Thursday of every May. This is a special day when every Christian in the United States of America is supposed to seek God's guidance and blessing on the good ol' U.S.A. Can you imagine how many prayers Shirley has to captain that day? As I said, I fear for her health. Shirley must feel on the first Friday in May like Santa Claus feels on December 26th.

How did the National Day of Prayer get started? I'm glad you asked.

In the summer of 1775, the Continental Congress realized that they needed God's help. It was very hot in Philadelphia then. Flies were buzzing around irritating everybody, and so was Ben Franklin. So the Continental Congress instituted the National Day of Prayer. The flies did not go away and Ben Franklin continued to be a nuisance, but this was only because the National Day of Prayer did not become official  until 1952, when Congress passed a joint resolution and Ben Franklin had died.

The law was amended in 1988, and from that year

forward, the first Thursday of May (not the second Thursday, not the first Wednesday, not the third Monday, not the first Saturday, but the first Thursday), was the day every Christian in America was supposed to pray for America.

Interesting sidetrack: I have done research and discovered that, while you are allowed to pray for America on the first Thursday of, say, June, it won't do any practical good. The whole idea of the National Day of Prayer is for Americans to pray to God simultaneously. Think of it this way: You can show up for a Monday Night Football game on Tuesday night, but how is this going to help your team? Or how will you buy a Coney dog? The question also arises: "What if I am an American citizen, but I am west of the International Date Line on, say, the island of Funafuti, during the National Day of Prayer?" Simple. Any place west of the International Date Line, including the island of Funafuti, is one day ahead of the United States. Therefore, you will pray for the United States on the first Friday of May. **This ends the interesting sidetrack.**

I don't know if this is still true because I don't really care, but in 1994, the United States was "the only country in the world with an official day of prayer." That's what the *Focus on the Family* magazine said. Seeing that, in 1994, the United States was, for forty-two years, the only country in the world with an official day of prayer,

I was amazed to find the following tidbit of information in the same February 1994 issue:

> We [the U.S.] are known as No. 1 in violent crime, No. 1 in divorce, No. 1 in teenage pregnancies in the Western world, No. 1 in voluntary abortions, No. 1 in illegal drug use, and No. 1 among industrial nations in illiteracy. There is no doubt our country is facing a desperate crisis.

Quoted on the same page, Shirley Dobson said, "Our society continues to deteriorate at an even more alarming pace."

This so astonished me that I made an extremely simple chart of what astonished me. Here is that chart:

If you have studied my chart carefully (and I hope you have), you can only reach one conclusion concerning the National Day of Prayer:

It don't work.

As a responsible, spirit-filled American, I am troubled by this. And so I have been banging my head against the wall since 1994 (don't try this at home; it hurts), attempting to figure out what has gone wrong with the National Day of Prayer. It can't be a numbers problem, because listen to this quote from page 2 of the February, 1994 edition of *Focus on the Family* magazine (I swear I'm not making this up):

> It is safe to say that the NDP, which was observed in more than 10,000 locales last year, had at least one million participants—and perhaps many millions—praying for our nation and its leaders. More minutes of prayer were directed to our heavenly Father than on any other day of the year, including Thanksgiving.

"Say Bill! Did ya hear? We broke the record!"

I researched this fantastic claim on the Internet (I may be making this up), discovering that, on Thanksgiving Day 1993, 127 minutes of prayer were directed to our heavenly Father. And yet, on the National Day of Prayer in 1994, one million participants prayed an average of 1/100 second each, resulting in a total prayer time of 166 minutes, beating the 1993 Thanksgiving Day total by 39 minutes.

Interesting sidetrack: You may wonder how millions of Americans praying on Thanksgiving Day could yield only 127 minutes of prayer. This figure is based on the average length of the traditional "blessing" said at American Thanksgiving dinner tables, which is, sur-prisingly, only 17 seconds. (Note: this is only the na-tional average. The length of Thanksgiving prayers in Massachusetts, for instance, is 35 seconds.) Also keep in mind that overlapping prayers do not count for ad-ditional time. For example, if there are four thousand prayers said between 2:00:00 and 2:00:17 p.m. E.S.T., this counts for only 17 seconds of actual prayer time. The 127 minute figure would be substantially lower were it not for our four time zones, which allow people to eat and pray at different times throughout the day. God blesses this nation, not because it is holy, but because it is wide. (Additional note: This explains why there are so many poor people in Chile.) **This ends the interest-ing sidetrack.**

So if it isn't a numbers problem, what is it? To find the answer, I went to the source of all answers, the Bible encyclopedia. But looking up "FAILED PRAYERS" there, I found: "See NATIONAL DAY OF PRAYER." So this did not help me.

But then I realized, *The Bible encyclopedia is not the source of all answers. The sacred scriptures are that.* So off I went to my Bible.

I looked up nearly fifty references on prayer until I found it: Elijah's challenge to the prophets of Baal to a prayer contest on Mt. Carmel. (Baal was a major false god back in Bible days.) Here, I felt, was the answer.

Elijah got lucky and won the contest, but the prophets of Baal had everything going for them. What happened? If I could discover why the prayers of these zealous prayer warriors failed, I would have some kind of clue as to how to remedy our National Day of Prayer.

For those unfamiliar with this account, there is no better description than the account itself. I quote from 1 Kings, chapter 18, from the New American Standard Bible. It's a lengthy passage, but it will reward your scrutiny:

> And Elijah came near to all the people and said, "How long will you hesitate between two opinions? If the Lord is God, follow Him; but if Baal, follow him." But the people did not answer him a word.
>
> Then Elijah said to the people, "I alone am left a prophet of the Lord, but Baal's prophets are 450 men. Now let them give us two oxen; and let them choose one ox for themselves and cut it up, and place it on the wood, but put no fire under it; and I will prepare the other ox, and lay it on the wood, and I will not put a fire under it. Then you call on the name of your god, and I will call on the name of the Lord, and the God who answers by fire, He is God."
>
> And all the people answered and said, "That is a good idea."
>
> So Elijah said to the prophets of Baal, "Choose one ox for yourselves and prepare it first for you are many, and call on the name of your god, but put no fire under it."

Then they took the ox which was given them and they prepared it and called on the name of Baal from morning until noon saying, "O Baal, answer us." But there was no voice and no one answered. And they leaped about the altar which they made.

And it came about at noon, that Elijah mocked them and said, "Call out with a loud voice, for he is a god; either he is occupied or gone aside, or is on a journey, or perhaps he is asleep and needs to be awakened."

So they cried with a loud voice and cut themselves according to their custom with swords and lances until the blood gushed out on them.

And it came about when midday was past, that they raved until the time of the offering of the evening sacrifice; but there was no voice, no one answered, and no one paid attention.

Then it came about at the time of the offering of the evening sacrifice, that Elijah the prophet came near and said, "Oh Lord, the God of Abraham, Isaac and Israel, today let it be known that Thou art God in Israel, and that I am Thy servant, and that I have done all these things at Thy word.

"Answer me, O Lord, answer me, that this people may know that Thou, O Lord, art God, and that Thou hast turned their heart back again."

Then the fire of the Lord fell, and consumed the burnt offering.

By analyzing this incident, I believe we will find answers to our national prayer woes.

First, you will notice that Elijah was only one man, while the prophets of Baal numbered 450. This would appear to uphold what we have already concluded, that one man in tune with God's will outperforms 450 morons who are not.

Slow down.

The spiritual leaders of the United States have already determined for us that we must pray as a nation. Don't you think they've studied it? Many of these men and women graduated with honors from the finest theological institutions in America. They have earned the most complicated degrees, some of which use five letters of the alphabet and mix capital letters with small letters. These educated men and women have already determined, through much study, that the more people praying for a thing (especially on the first Thursday in

"Why the hell did you pray on Friday instead of Thursday? Damn it, Fred, you're ruining this country."

May), the more God is bound to listen and act.

Second, just who was this Elijah? Ancient Bible encyclopedias paint for us a country bumpkin from the desert crossroads of Tishbe. Elijah did not possess even one degree from one accredited theological institution. Some Bible historians now believe that Elijah never even made it out of the eighth grade.

Did Elijah, then, simply get lucky on Carmel?

Since it was the prophets of Baal, and not Elijah, who had so much going for them (the numbers, the zeal, the volume, the prayer-time), what went wrong?

From reading and rereading the passage, it seems obvious to me now that the prophets stopped too soon. Note: the prophets of Baal, "raved until the time of the offering of the evening sacrifice." This is precisely the time when prayer becomes most effective, as we have already seen with many of the ALL NIGHT PRAYER VIGILS springing up in serious-minded churches across America.

I am suspicious that Elijah picked just this time to interrupt the prophets. I believe that Elijah wished to tire his opponents, to wear them out before the critical ALL NIGHT PRAYER VIGIL, when the prophets of Baal would certainly have prevailed.

When did the contest slip from the Baalmen's grasp? I believe it was when they allowed Elijah to coax them from their game plan. Like George Foreman, who let

Mohammed Ali "rope-a-dope" him into exhaustion in "The Rumble in the Jungle," the prophets of Baal let Elijah draw them from their comfort zone with his cruel mocking. And this, in the last three rounds.

Just as in boxing, proper physical training is crucial to any prayer enterprise. And this is the very thing that the leaders of the National Day of Prayer have neglected. This, I believe, is the missing element, the correction of which will right our intercessional wrongs.

I am not the sort of person who fingers other people's failings, then runs. I have a solution, and it is this: Take all that the prophets of Baal did right, then refine these elements with specific exercises that will increase both strength and stamina.

And so, it is as a concerned American citizen and a very spiritual person, that I offer to my countrymen and women (and to any individuals around the world who wish to adopt the program, including Canadians): *Martin Zender's Complete Prayer Training Program.*

The Mt. Carmel Leap
Purpose: To develop the muscles in the front of the legs and the calves.

Motive: To leap high and lengthily in prayer. The prophets of Baal "leaped about the altar which they had made." No wonder they got tired. How long do you think an untrained person can keep this up? This exer-

"We worked up to twenty-five repetitions of the
Mt. Carmel Leap in only three weeks!"

cise will turn a "morning-until-noon" leaper into a
twenty-four-hour jumping machine.

The exercise: Stand with feet comfortably apart.
Grasp one three-pound rock in each hand. Let arms
hang naturally at sides. Bend both knees and lower yourself until thighs are parallel to floor. Leap into air as
high as possible and try to land without hurting yourself.

Repetitions: Start with ten, then increase repetitions
by five jumps a week for eight weeks.

The Larynx Blaster

Purpose: To strengthen the organ in the throat that
facilitates shouting.

Motive: To be able to shout to God louder and
longer. The prophets of Baal "called on the name of
Baal from morning until noon." Up until this time, the
Baalmen shouted well within themselves. But at noon,
Elijah mocked them and said, "Call out with a loud

voice, for he is a god; either he is occupied or gone aside, or is on a journey, or perhaps he is asleep and needs to be awakened." This led to the prophets' undoing. Spurred to volumes beyond their fitness level, the Baalmen "cried with a loud voice" and eventually contracted laryngitis. Eight weeks of The Larynx Blaster would have prevented this.

The exercise: Stand with feet shoulder's width apart. Place a friend three cubits away. If the friend's name is Steuben, say, "Hey Steuben!" If Steuben can hear you, this is one repetition. Place Steuben six cubits away and repeat. Repeat at three-cubit intervals until Steuben says, "*Huh?*" This is enough for one day.

Repetitions: Perform exercise daily until Steuben can hear you at 100,000 cubits. This is approximately the distance from Jerusalem to Jericho. Allow eight weeks for improvement.

Bent-Over Consciousness Rows

Purpose: To improve the oxygen-carrying capability of the blood.

Motive: To maintain consciousness even while missing half your blood supply. The prophets of Baal executed a reliable prayer technique: bloodletting. But once again, they failed to properly gauge their fitness level. "They cried with a loud voice and cut themselves according to their custom with swords and lances until the blood gushed out on them." But the account doesn't tell us how many Baalmen passed out. Bible historians now believe that probably half of the 450 who began the competition never made it to the lances. Baal hates it when that happens. My Bent-Over Consciousness Rows would have prevented this disaster.

The exercise: Stand with feet shoulder's width apart. Grasp one three-pound rock in each hand, letting arms hang naturally at sides. Have a training partner sever your carotid artery with a sword and drain half (1/2) of your blood supply. Bend over until your head is six inches above your heart. Let rocks hang below your knees, but do not let them touch the ground. Be sure to keep your knees slightly bent! Lift rocks to your chest. Lower rocks. This, unfortunately, is only one repetition.

Repetitions: Perform twenty repetitions of this exercise, or as many as you can perform before passing out. When first beginning this exercise, many people find themselves losing consciousness after only two or three repetitions. Be patient and do not become discouraged. After eight weeks, you will be able to perform the required repetitions. At this point, you may wish to increase the weight of the rocks. **Important note:** Never remove more than half your blood supply!

The Rave
Purpose: To strengthen the muscles of the mouth

that cause a person to talk wildly.

Motive: The more syllables you can press into one breath, the more God will realize how badly you want all the things you want. We read that the prophets of Baal "raved until the time of the offering of the evening sacrifice." Had the prophets raved beyond that time, Baal would have heard them for the sheer prolongedness of their multisyllabacy; yes, they would have "broken through" to the blessed life. Obviously, the Baalmen desyllablized far short of their goal. This does not have to happen to you.

The exercise: Stand with feet shoulder's width apart. Begin raving. If you cannot think of anything to rave about, a training partner can assist you. Have your partner remind you how dissatisfied you are with your lot in life. Things like, "Jerry's house is bigger than yours," "The Johnson's car makes yours look like crap," and "Your wage is far below the national average," work well. As you begin to rave, have your training partner count the number of syllables you utter per second. Continue raving for one minute. Rest. Repeat, this time while looking out the window at the Johnsons' car.

Repetitions: Perform The Rave only once a day. Any more than this may cause a precipitous rise in blood pressure, and you will not be able to do your Bent-Over Consciousness Rows.

NOTE: Anyone can perform The Rave. Beginners, however, may wish to build up to their first Rave slowly.

When you pray, don't be like the play-actors. They love to stand and pray in the synagogues and at street-corners so that people may see them at it. Believe me, they have had all the reward they are going to get. But when you pray, go into your own room, shut your door and pray to your Father privately. Your Father who sees all private things will reward you. And when you pray don't rattle off long prayers like the pagans who think they will be heard because they use so many words. Don't be like them. For your Father knows your needs before you ask him.

—*Jesus Christ,* Matthew 6:5-9

These recommendations from Jesus graduate from flesh to spirit, from exercise to rest.

Note first how Jesus says not to pray in public like a bunch of hams. He says go to your room instead and have a private time with God. This way, you can pour out your agonies and thanksgivings to Him without style points or curtain calls.

Then Jesus says not to rattle off long prayers like pagans. Apparently, pagans think that words are like points that rack up digitally on a pinball machine. Yet this is exactly what the Catholic church told me to do: Pray this many prayers and you'll rack up points, which to the Catholics meant having your sins forgiven. It was words that counted. More words, longer words, better words. I had to say so many of this prayer, so many of that. So many prayers and I'd get an extra ball, or a bonus round. Saying the rosary was like getting your metal ball stuck in a metal hole, when the machine just goes wild. Bells ring, lights flash, and you're sitting there going, "Oh, God, I'm racking up the points now!" God's eyes light up and He must be saying to the angels, "Holy Moses, this guy's headed for a single-game record."

The National Day of Prayer people care mainly about two things: 1) the number of people praying, and 2) the number of minutes prayed. In my opinion, these kinds of people are worse than Third World Jungle Pagans. At least Third World Jungle Pagans don't white-wash their pagan practices with Jesus' name. Not even Third World Jungle Pagans are that audacious. Third World Jungle Pagans stand there with their tongues hanging out and their naked bodies bloodied and dirt-caked from God-knows-what, but you just don't get the impression that they're looking at the unconverted and thinking, *Why aren't you doing this, friend? This is what Jesus would do. Why don't you be like me so God will bless our nation? You don't want to go to hell, do you?*

Jesus contrasts babbling with, "Your Father knows your needs before you ask him." This is real progress, when you graduate from syllables to silence. This knowing that God already knows comes very close to not actually saying anything to God, but simply relaxing in Him, knowing He's got things under control. Rest in prayer comes from wanting only what God wants, going only where God wants to go. I'm very interested in this kind of prayer. I think it's prayer's highest form.

Never stop praying.
—*the Apostle Paul,* 1 Thessalonians 5:17

How the heck can you not stop praying? Did Paul actually mean this? I think that he did. I think this is the high form of prayer I just mentioned. I think the highest "forms" of prayer involve rest, when you're not actually doing or saying anything.

The NDP people would never see it this way. The NDP, naturally misreading this verse, would distribute toothpicks to keep everyone's eyes open. But that's not what Paul is talking about here. It can't be.

The highest form of prayer involves realization and trust—realization that we don't know what's best, and trust that God does. This makes me think of something else Paul said:

The Spirit also helps us in our present limitations. For example, we do not know how to pray worthily, but his

Spirit within us is actually praying for us in those agonizing longings which cannot find words.

—Romans 8:26

Agonizing longings that cannot find words. That's me. Limitations. That's me, too. Paul's got me pegged here. This is me, all of it. I'm so messed up some days that I don't know my rear end from a light socket. I'm confused, disoriented, mad. I don't know what to do, what to pray for, nothing. I have no confidence. Who am I to know what God wants? Who am I to even ask God for something? I know who I am, I know what I am. I'm a weak lump of clay, whereas, God is God. There's contrast for you. How's that for a contrast? Do you like that contrast? A weak lump of clay versus God. Is that contrast enough for you? How dare I assume to know what God wants—unless He tells me in scripture.

So why not let God pray? Why not let God's spirit in me pray with an intelligence that I don't have? It's smart, I'm not. Here, finally, is something I can attain to.

"Where's Martin?"

"Oh, he's praying."

"But he's over there sleeping on the couch."

"I know."

Lloyd Sumner of Charlottesville, Virginia, rode his bicycle around the world. Yep. All the way around, including his passage from India to Africa on the good ship *Harsha Vardhana*. Sumner explains:

The *Harsha Vardhana* was only one-third full, which meant nobody objected when I rode around one of the decks every day to stay in shape. This deck cycling was especially thrilling when the ship rolled to the ocean's swells. By carefully timing my turns at each side, I never stopped coasting. It was a cyclist's dream, downhill, downhill forever.
        —excerpted from *The Long Ride*, published by Stackpole Books. Copyright 1978 by Lloyd Sumner.

What a picture of unceasing prayer. God's will is the ocean, rolling where it will. The person who wants to pray without stopping first reads the dips and swells, then times his "ride" to the beat of the water. The rewards are pleasant, for one "never stops coasting," even as one does no work. Fighting the waves, however, carries consequences. Sumner again:

One day I'd coasted almost an hour when I misjudged the ship's roll and crashed into a post. A sharp pain pierced my right side, and I feared I'd broken some ribs.

The National Day of Prayer sits limp in a wheelchair with a chestful of bandages. This is the price of misjudging the waves. What does *God* want? It's a very good question. No one has asked it in two thousand and fifteen years.

When the sail controls the wind, when the rudder controls the sea, only then will the hand of humanity move the great arm of God.

And *this* is the boldness which we have toward Him, that if we should be requesting anything according to His will, He is hearing us.

—1 John 5:14

MEDIA
WINNERS
CIRCLE

How To QUIT CHURCH Without Quitting God

I NOW WANTED TO ESCAPE THE BOX

martin zender

"This is the best book I have ever read in my life."

Patricia Spears

"A provocative, irreverent and intellectual romp. You need to read this book."

Dwight Green
Ft. Worth Star-Telegram

"For anyone who feels caught in the rut of church."

Dan Julian
MSU State News

Is Jesus Christ a Christian?
Is "going to church" in the Bible?
Why can't I get straight answers in church?
Does God love people who don't love Him?
Why is Christian television so stupid?
Is it wrong to question the organized church?
Are my gut instincts about God scriptural?
How does Satan operate today?
AND MORE

"You'll try like crazy to prove him wrong."

Bible Time
America News

Escape the Box.

186 pages. Hardcover.

Toll-free ordering: 1-866-866-BOOK

**Or send $19.95 plus $4.00 shipping to:
Starke & Hartmann P.O. Box 6473
Canton, OH 44706**

Or order online at: www.starkehartmann.com

"God used this small book
to change my life.
After fifteen years
in the pulpit, I finally
understand what hell is.
Better late than never."

--J. Marcus Oglesby,
M.Div.

Martin Zender
Goes To Hell

A critical look at an uncriticized doctrine.

At last. Here are the facts.

"Why has it taken so long for someone
to write a book like this? Thank God
for Martin Zender!"   *--Jeannie Moore*

100 pages. Paperback. Available now.

starkehartmann.com Toll Free: 1-866-866-BOOK

Want more of Martin?

Articles. Essays. Photos. Audio clips.

*"Batten down your
stained-glass hatches."*

www.martinzender.com

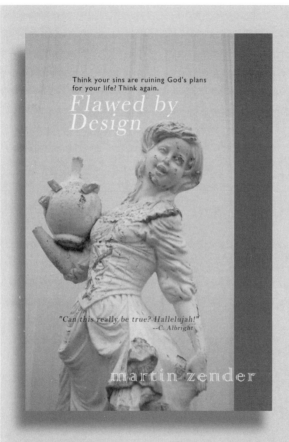

Think your sins are ruining God's plans for your life? Think again.

Flawed by Design

"Can this really be true? Hallelujah!"
--C. Albright

martin zender

"This is Martin Zender's best book yet. Period."
Ryan Doershuck
New York Writer's Group

1 - 8 6 6 - 8 6 6 - B O O K
w w w . s t a r k e h a r t m a n n . c o m